MEMOIR OF CRUSHED PETALS

i

MEMOIR OF CRUSHED PETALS

Pamilerin Jacob

WORDS
RHYMES &
RHYTHM

Printed and Published in Nigeria by:
Words Rhymes & Rhythm Limited
Suite C309, Global Plaza Plot 366,
ObafemiAwolowo Way, Jabi District, Abuja,
Nigeria.
08169027757, 08060109295
www.wrr.ng

for **Durojaiye** *(wait, and enjoy life),*
you never waited...

Contents

the first question 1

the myth of joy 3

Rain 4

the myth of joy I..6

the myth of joy II 8

the myth of joy III..10

the psychology of sadness 11

4am..13

a smile is a stain...14

my bible, my skin 15

cracked eggs never heal 17

to Khalil 18

yams and misfortune......................................20

trance 22

You 24

intrusive thoughts 26

real men 27

feelings: four poems.......................................29

feelings: images of me 30

mirror...32

elegy for bliss 34

this body..37

cremation 38

some other questions.....................................43

sos..44

caesura 46

on why I write...47

to my placenta 48

the welder 49

schizophrenia...50

orison for lightning.......................................51

abiku's monologue 54

abiku's monologue 55

songs of woe 59

song 0 60

song I...61

song II 63

song III...65

song IV 67

song V..68

song VI 70

thorns and petals...71

rose 72

thorns and petals............................74

aina..75

dinner 78

brain freeze 79

water has a voice 81

r&b: rape & beg 84

no..86

to the little one in Syria 87

how to forget your heritage............88

profession of faith 89

the first question

god, do you love me?

the myth of joy

"My own soul bites into itself,
like a scorpion ringed with fire"
- Ankh-f-n-khonsu

Rain

I popped out of the womb
like a tablet from its cocoon,
my first language, a syntax of tears-
laughter has become a chore, like pushing
a truck stuck in mire

life grabs my heel like a midwife,
spanks me for not crying loud enough,
for having decibels lower than thunder
and I, upside down like a bat
have salt gathering beneath my eyes, have
blood gathering in the pouch of my forehead;
a boil:

boil bursts, and
my eyes turn sprinklers for sorrow-
now, thunders bellow beneath my tongue

and on some days, when god washes his hands
into the clouds, when the palm leaves begin to
shiver
I am flung into a poem, to be cuddled by fire
ahhhh!…I like how fire snuggles one,
how it walks upon the skin with nails
in its soles
shoving memories beneath scars
how it pops the eyeballs like pimples,

I like how the sky declares her love
for the earth

how she whips the forest with lightning
and ecstasy
all in one------------stroke
reminds me of a masquerade
that appears in every dream,

whispering
to me
every night it rains, that daemon-

a masquerade
whose penis size I wish to forget...

there are many accusers
who don the veil of trust,
poking me on all sides with words
whetted on the edge of bedtime secrets,
"look at you
creaming your body with faeces
'cause you wouldn't
let go of shit…"

where do you think
ants go to become soldiers,
how do tongues gain
the precision of arrows,

sometimes the accusers say I am possessed
of four hundred and eighteen daemons,
"he needs deliverance, haven't you seen him
lip-syncing to the tremolo of the legion,
how he cuts his skin,
with blades and knives"

but when the deliverer sees me,
he picks up his heels, and places them on his head
in hot escape,
like a grasscutter running from a dog-
he says my eyes have arrows for pupils
that every scar on my body is a confession
written by demons who wish to enter heaven

often, I look out the window for joy

but I see the orange seller touching her toes,
a piece of raggedy foam in her mouth
to silence her screams- an idiot
jerking behind her like a diseased cock-

she is thirteen

the myth of joy II

chief priest:
my teeth are soft like marshmallows
I am tired of chewing
I am tired of chewing my own vomit

the stars said to me, "cast your stones
upon the river, they will float"
the river echoed the same,
so I cast my first son into the river,
he did not float…
babies do not float, even after swimming for
nine moons in the maternal pond

in grief, I picked cowries off the bed
of the river while the waves slept,
I ate them, one by one by one by one
all seven of them, until I heard god scream
in my oesophagus-
god does not speak, until you pinch him
sorrow is a dumb parrot, until you laugh

if you eat ash long enough, it
will begin to taste like salt

my teeth have become marshmallows
and my tongue is a wilting leaf-
it will fall out of my mouth,
when god stops screaming:

I want to laugh, I want to, but

I do not know how to vomit right,
where do I pour my grief
into a cup, into a quill,
or do I chew until my teeth dissolves into milk?

often, when I ponder on the conundrum
the mountains begin to yell, they tell me to speak
that in speaking, sorrow seeps out the edges of the
lips
that it leaps from the withered tongue into the air

these mountains are liars, for when mountains speak
when they spew violent thoughts upon green leaves,
when mountains attempt to laugh
sorrow does not leap into the air- permanently-
it settles upon the forehead of the earth
as fire on the skin of the sun-

ancestors, tell me
why is sorrow so clingy,
why is joy so distant
why is sorrow addictive
and joy repugnant:

I swallowed the stones
one by one by one by one,
let every mountain hold its tongue
and every accuser swallow his thoughts

the myth of joy III

moss gathers around
my eyes, thick like hair

    and tears meander through
like a motorcycle
    finding its way
in a traffic jam

I poke the winds with my fingers
in search of joy:

joy is the space
behind my ears
I will never see…

the psychology of sadness

moments are batons handed over
from minute to minute
each running with fractured legs
a memory ticks, the tongue talks
scatters words like ashes unto serene waters

say to self, *this body is alien*
these veins look like ropes,
I should tie them round my neck
and tighten...

memory is a trickster,
it paints the tongue with wishes
memory swallows salt
soaks up water like a sponge

memory is a bucket
with perforated bottom,
we pour heaps of sand into it
it gives us stones

some moments take off the coat
of memory and we are left
to stare into the eyes of our reflection
-in water- as we divine

we speak happiness into existence
with our middle finger in the anus
of the air

beg sorrow to get out of our skins

by slicing it open

we repeat
we repeat
we reap it

the fruits of sadness
hiding in our bones

4am

the moon a pimple glows
on the forehead of the sky-
heavy with pus, with hypnotic light

I want to burst it,
wash my face with liquid light
want to crush it with my elbows,
so the pus splashes into my mouth

4am. a pimple glows on my cheek
in the dark
like a rosary bead

awaiting the touch of your silky tentacles
to caress conscience into deep sleep

as you sneak into forbidden crevices,
forcefully…

morning: I wake up to a voice
begging me
for water. my tongue is a sound
caught in my mouth

I withdraw from bed, the way
a snail withdraws (from life) into shell
my bed is a colony of misery
when you cry long enough
your pillow learns to carry
weights too heavy for the head-
turns to stone.

I am tired of lying to self:
say, a smile is a stain
on the face of a sad man
say, a tear is the soul's manner
of speech, an algorithm of salt

night: I see two lizards
making out beside my bed
I crush their skulls with my shoe

I hear children screaming
in the next room. two of them.

I am still thirsty…

my bible, my skin

the pages of my bible are black
like my skin-
my skin is wholly sin

(so I've been told...)

in my bible are dead flowers
warm, like the forehead of a teething child-
but even dead leaves have chlorophyll
and fallen feathers become quills

are stories not bees, leaping from tongue
to ear in search of warmth,
is my skin not a leaf hanging from the tip
of my father's penis

the cleric says to flip the scriptures
so I stick a knife into my flesh-
has the word not been made flesh, black flesh...?

in my skin are dead flowers
straining their ears for the voice of the sun
the sun whispers a myth, drops an hieroglyphic
into my palms

so I run, I run

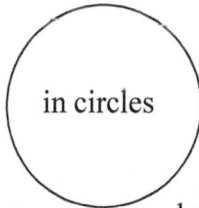
in circles

in search of   meaning,
until a tornado   is birthed
and dead flowers   leap out of my skin

15

as butterflies- I am a cocoon-

inscribed on their wings are answers
to every question,
but I cannot see, I cannot see them
through the veil of dust beclouding my eyes

the veil of thoughts, of dos and don'ts:
don't be depressed, don't ever tell them you are
depressed
do remember to hide your pain under your armpits
Nigerians are never depressed; it is the white man's
disease

don't be a fucking bastard…!

cracked eggs never heal

*"I have seen a candle flame
on the navel of my grave"*
-   Servio Gbadamosi

*"Perhaps I should wrap this hope
with rag and put it under sand"*
-   Obari Gomba

to Khalil

dear Khalil,
today
I found termites in my blood

and in my bone
marrow,
a vineyard of worms

feasting

as the unripe man goes
cold, lying bare
upon the breastplate of dust
like unripe mangoes,

awaiting the call of a mute gong
in the hands of an impotent clock:

cock crows.　　man grows.　　man goes.

death sentences are long sentences with half-baked
commas and charred full stopsssssssssssssssss

burning the tongue of doctors,　　　"we care, god
heals…
　　　~~kills too sometimes~~"

what if you sliced open a banana
and met a testicle,

what if raindrops were a sign, that
heaven is melting,

what if you poked your eyes with broken bottles
and heard the cries of little children
-foetuses screaming in the uterus
of your eye sockets-

what if crickets were wraiths
mourning their own deaths,
-taking turns to groan each night
because their throats are clogged
with sin; with the liquid flames of hell-

what if, question marks were fragments of a rope
binding the legs of answers

- **these questions bumped into me
in my sleep**

yams and misfortune

I

these days, the walls have stopped whispering
lizards have stopped nodding, and
when I clasp my hands to pray, I hear angels
hissing-

angels, I betrothed my milk teeth to
angels who learnt to worship god
by listening to me

last night, I sat in my reading chair,
and it
          crumbled
like a pillar of sand punched by the wind
soldier ants have eaten into the pith of my chair,
now I totter- on the floor-
back into memories that have no taste
and forth into days, lined with vinegar-
where does a smile learn to bend its back?

II

last week, my *bestie* called me an onion
said every time I open my heart, people cry
who is to blame for the misfortune of the yam

the farmer said to the yam,
"peel your skin, peel your skin
all your lovers are dead because your skin
is laced with madness, and
every time they touch you, they are cursed to

scratch   scratch scratch
until blood gushes out of their soul"

the yam did not know,
that the farmer had furnished his pot with spices
that saints are permitted to lie, as long as
it is for the sake of righteousness-

feeding the family is an act of righteousness
depression can be righteous too, like cancer
it can be purified of stigma, if angels agree
to be baptized in the waters of wisdom

who is to blame for the misfortune
of the yam,
but the earth who forgot to teach the yam
to love itself?

I:
??? ??? ???   ??? ??? ???
???   ???   ???
??? ??? ???   ??? ??? ???
        ???   ???
        ???   ???
??? ??? ???   ??? ??? ???

??????
?????? logos...
??????

selah

2:45am,
when the orifice of consciousness splits
like lips parting slowly for a kiss,
I stare into the lambent flame of Nuit
into her eyes as she rasps-

seated on the laps of Aquinas, she hums:
1. god is the tree of first cause
2. depression is a leaf
3. god nourishes depression
then she puts her tongue into my mouth,
and words
words seep out like albumen from the shell
of a cracked egg-
cracked eggs never heal-
she rasps on,

"I am malnourished because
god loves to mask sorrow
as a test:
kill your son, slice your wrists
swallow office pins, swallow
the masquerade's penis…

trust me, I will give your stars
for children if you obey me,
when you slice your wrists
I will turn your blood into wine,
we will drink of it together
then will I turn you into dust

so you can ride the winds
like a vicious bull

so you can bash your head
into the iris of emptiness
'curse god and die'- a trap
how do you curse a curse...

simply love him, he is bereaved
he is a child with weak limbs,
a tree with sick leaves

god is love 'because a man said so,

man is the tree of noble cause
twisted, beaten
eating of god's grief-stricken leaves
out of love"

Nuit pulls her tongue out
of my mouth,
but cracked eggs never heal, and
bellicose words have been spewed
into the pouch of conscience

3:17am.

You

u, every time I see you
I want to throw up
into a calabash

then spread it as butter
on agege bread for you to eat

or maybe use it to
wash your face
-apply morning and evening
like Nixoderm
for optimum effect-

or maybe add it to
your indomie-
as per secret ingredient-

or keep it in the freezer
so when it is iced, you
throw it into a gallon of kunu, and drink

nothing tastes better than puke
and bad memories, you know…

there are many flavours of misery
but you, you are my favourite
you are pain made flesh

u,
every time I look into your eyes

you remind me of a bird
born without wings

whose nest is on fire
a bird singing elegies for its own soul
with an arrow in its tongue

(walks away from the mirror)

intrusive thoughts

every time, I walk past the transformer
I hear my name,

sizzling in between
naked wires

death is thinking of me...

death,
is in love with me...

real men

five
four
three
two

O
N
E:

crush. I will tell my lover- tonight-
to crush my testicles
like palm kernels

so my unborn children will learn
the anecdote of pain
by heart,
so my penis will learn
the eulogy of Darwin before
touching the walls of a vagina

5,   4
three times, I called my mother
to tell her about it
but every time the phone rang
I saw her bathing in ashes,
mourning, afternoon, night; mourning
tapping *the navel of my grave*
with her breasts, "god, why me,
why did you give me this child
only to snatch him from me
like a robber?"-   weird vision.

five,   4
3
two days ago, I saw a snail sniffing
salt like coke,
he had no shell, I asked him why
he had chosen to forsake himself, why
he had chosen to swallow fire

he told me, shells were for weaklings
that real men eat poison and don't die, that
real men will never ever ever ever ever ever ever
ever cry
even when you crush their testicles

"really?"
"yea, for reals"

five,   four
three, two…
I will tell my lover to buy a pair of scissors
instead, why crush my testicles
when we can cut them off
and make eggrolls with them

when we can stuff the eye of my penis
with many broomsticks
to test the limit of my *manliness*

feelings: four poems

loneliness is…
standing in the crowd
talking to stones

pain is…
Big Aunty poking your flaccid
penis for one more erection

emptiness is…

love is…
a drop of water on the tongue
after a seven-day fast

feelings: images of me

*"it is better to produce one image in a lifetime,
than to produce voluminous works"*
-     *Ezra Pound*

a coin dipped in conc. acid,
a puppy kicked in the head

ghana must go sack
set ablaze, ~~naira notes~~
politicians screaming

a standing fan
(with fresh breath, triune tongue
cooling the room)
sweating

wet mud, sitting in the oven
knife dipped in fire, red
like mother's tongue

sliced plantain
in the mouth of a skillet, howling
in hot groundnut oil

ice cream cup facedown
in sand, bleeding

an earthworm in the beak
of a bird
a shirt without buttons

corn seed in the gullet
of a broiler
a prisoner, counting his toes

a bald woman,
a snake crawling in front
of the hunter

your lover's footsteps, waning
an egg falling out
of the nest,
a nest without eggs,

hairless monkey,
a light bulb- at night-
without insects

unpicked meat in the pot,
a guitar without strings

a fan with one blade,
hair in a barber's shop,
an unmarked grave:

what if feathers were leaves
who refused to die,

and birds were trees
who learnt to fly?

some days, I look into the mirror
to reassert my existence

say my eye is a candle
melting every time my soul is afire

say, my pain is tasty
so I serve it in a bowl of poems
-to my readers-

say, I sit with Silence,
and watch her
slaughter a dove

say, I run naked into the mirror
in search of myself:

oh, where do you feel the pain?
everywhere

my soul is a balloon
floating upwards
in a room of stalactites

say, death is a parasite
eating up my thoughts

say, my sole has encountered
a colony
of fire ants,

say, my words are hollow
and tongue-searing

I swear to pain,
the mirror is a lake

I want to crawl
to the
                    bottom
and sleep there...

elegy for bliss

I
bliss, please, cease
your wailing,

my ears are tired of your songs
they are furled like padimo[1]

I am tired. I am tired.
wo, otisu mi![2]

every time I pass beside your grave
I hear you struggling, kicking
screaming, hissing,
you hear my footsteps
and start to gobble my name like a turkey
you wheeze, you sneeze,
you shriek

but I don't care

you have been tucked in bed
for an eternal sleep
close your eyes, yield

II
bliss, is it true
that I am a glitch?

---

[1] Mimosa pudica: a plant whose leaves furl when touched
[2] See, I am tired.

34

bliss, who do you talk to when
you are sad,

what is the colour of happiness?

how do you tickle
the river- I hear it laughing every day-

bliss,
am I really a glitch?

bliss, please,
answer me…

III
fifteen years now, since you stopped   c   o   o   i
n   g
in my ears
today, I finished baptismal class
so we went to the river for a ~~swim:~~

*"I baptize you in the name of the father,
son and…"*
I saw your face under the water
why did you wear my mother's face?

the priest pulled me out like an eagle
a fish, he stole me from the vision

after church, I ran to your grave
and met palm oil smeared on the stone
like dried stain on a white shirt-

someone
has been feeding you

iblis[3],
someone has been feeding you

---

[3] The Devil

this body

this body is not mine.
memory is a casket.

how do you walk into the past
without scratching your soul

how does a bone break
under the weight of air

this body is an abandoned house.
I see roaches sprawling
in between my toes,
they submit their wings in my palms
refuse to eat of my clothes

they want a taste of my innards
want to know what sorrow tastes like:
so I stick a fork into my elbow
to let them in…

cremation

I: omens
there are omens falling
like tears from the eye of fate
to warn me, the forlorn -

in the bathroom
brown leaves fall out of the shower head
instead of water,

in the kitchen
when I dip my hand into a jar of salt
I pull out a worm, warm
twitching like a chopped off limb

in my room
I hear rats squealing at 3:17am,
I reach under my pillow for my bible
-psalm 60 should come in handy today-
but I meet cowries, two blue cowries
I dust them off my bed in fear, midair
they become roaches and fly
into my ears-
the rats stop squealing

in church
when I am told to share the grace
I reach into my pocket for it
but pull out a penis, a masquerade's penis
everybody starts to laugh, then they start to cry
an elder walks up to me, grabs my ankle

and threatens to chop it off
but I know, I know
he is a masquerade too

fire, you liar
you cannot hurt me

fate, wipe your eyes with your knuckles
crack your fingers, and strum me a lullaby
on your lyre
for a every matchstick I swallow

fire, you liar
swallow these omens
instead of me

II: questions
if I hold my palm over a flame
will it melt,

if it melts, what melts first
my thumb or my index

what about the hairs beneath my knuckles
and the lines on my palm

if I hold my palm over a flame
will it burn brighter
if I pour my blood into fire
who dies-me or the flame-

what would you do,

if you met fire inside a coconut
instead of water

would you still shake it,
would you shake it and throw it
into the compound of your enemy

can water die,
is fire the first son of the wind
who is the last born of the wind

can I die,

if I hold my palm over a flame
will it melt?

III: fire
I hold a story in my palms
waiting for it to mature
my life, chapter of omens
awaiting fulfillment of prophecy

if I hold my palm over a flame
will it…

fire calls me son, fire calls me
many things,
fire is the farmer with a basketful of omens
fire is oxygen that escaped the fetters of water
fire is not my father, fire is a masquerade

fire bites me without teeth, fire loves

my skin, my naked skin
fire likes to speak in tongues
fire is not my father

I hold a story in my palms
waiting for it to mature
but fire hates stories,
fire tells me to die by fire

fire is a masquerade
fire is not my father

IV: ashes
in the genealogy of memories
my first kiss was with fire

in the vineyard of truth
my first kiss was a lie

how long does it take to melt
before a flame

does a candle rejoice when it
sees the match,
does a match rejoice when it
sees its mother

how do you chase your dreams
with boils, living in between your toes

I heard once the lore
of how the moon tied a string to the testicles
of the ocean,

and pulled it daily, like an obdurate ram
until it burst into waves

how do you chase a dream
melting into fear, like vitamin c on your tongue
how do you run when the moon chases you
with a leash?

how do you tell the story of fire
to a garden, decked in dew?

when fire burns me to ashes
and I am scattered in the ocean of untold stories
will the waves comfort me,

will death comfort me?

some other questions

I

what do you call the wind
that gathers in your lungs
when you cry?

what do you call a sigh
that rests on the shoulder
of a smile?

what do you call a miracle
that refuses
to crawl out of god's palm?

what do you do when you
call, but your words
fall like pebbles into the sea
unheard?

II

who will console the scarecrow
in love with a bird?

how did the moon get its rashes?

what do shadows say to each other
when they meet?

who leads the orchestra of frogs
every night?

(to afrovikky)

I
dear afrovikky,
my soul is heavy with anguish,
my mind nests tornadoes

pneuma is wind, pneuma is spirit
spirit is wind. I want to be light
like the wind
to dance to sweet songs in my dreams

my body is a cylinder, and
my spirit is trapped
in between cells

I am paper, every
breath I take
is a pair of scissors
slicing me

II
do you know my tongue
breaks into nightmares
every time I smile

do you know on each finger

misery sits
and sings to me

do you know my tears
-when I hold them to my nostrils-
smell
of death?

III
I am the High Priest of death

my shoulders collapse
like foam
every time sorrow perches,

in my chest
black blood gathers:

how does a heart pump
when it is clogged
with the whispers of ghosts?

Reply (Dec 1, 12:37pm):
Hi Jacob,
I need you to arrange your thoughts;
that's all I need you to do
put them in folders, and keep them

in a safe place till we can talk,
can you do that for me?

caesura

out of my mind bled a stain,
that gave joy to the sane and
insane
- Olatunde Chidera Obafemi

every day, death is postponed
because
of an unfinished poem

on why I write

I miss you…

to my placenta

the welder

I carry my bones
to the welder, tell him
to join my pieces together
make a collage of my mistakes

art… fart

whichever.
it depends on the nose that smells it

inside of me a cock crows at midnight,
its throat is the long hand
of a clock that runs on blood

I am drying up,
sorrow licks me up
as a cat licks milk

the welder throws sand in my eyes
says to me, *"I only join pieces that fit,*
you, Pamilerin,
you smell of misfortune"

I walk away:
a river laden with faeces
and dead fishes

wishing for canoes
wishing

some days,
the man in the mirror
smiles at me

he is not me

schizophrenia

orison for lightning

- the chief priest
pulls out the little finger of an infant
with pincers- the child does not cry-
and with it, touches his forehead, his chest and his
navel
then he licks the blood, and lifts up the finger to the
wind-

chief priest:
lightning, necklace of the gods
come have a bite of this meal, this
little finger; like chin chin

lightning, why are you angry?
why do you always fall off the
edge of the cloud when it rains?

lightning, you who is silent as a snail
forerunner of thunder, swifter than a sneeze.
come have a bite of this meal, this
little finger; like kuli kuli

(sky darkens, the chief priest begins to chant)

I am a river, I am a river
let every debris in my path
obey my voice

I am a cyclone, a fat cyclone
let every tree clench their teeth

51

in fear of me

a wire, no matter how it coils
can never be a snake
the wind, regardless of its speed
will never grow legs

I am a river, I am a cyclone
I am a fiery cyclone howling
like a man kicked in the balls

lightning, strike my chest
with your axe, lightning
strike your axe upon my head

when a bubble dies, the laundryman
is unmoved
when I die, may the earth wait one minute
in orbit

lightning, I have called you by name
I have called you by name
I have called you by name,

do not hes------i------tate

(turns to the infant)
Ego,
I see you are bruised, your nerves
eaten up by cankerworms- you feel nothing

I see you looking,
but I know you see nothing

you are a mirror with one reflection,
you show only pain

I hate you, I hate you
as dry feet hate hot coals
I hate you, I hate you
as a cube of sugar hates water

I feel no---------thing because,
you are.

you are grease spilled onto the paper
of my joy,
I cannot wash you off.

I hate you, Self
you are what I am,

you are all I am...

abiku's monologue

abiku's monologue

I: the meeting
mother should never have taken that route
to the market, the one covered in dead snails
eggshells, and lizard tails-
maybe, she would not have met me

I remember walking on the edge of a leaf
with my fingers that day, when her skirt
brushed against the blade of the grass;
she had tripped over a stone, and I
falling off the leaf, leapt over her legs

Eewo! Taboo!
I, a mosquito pulled into the vortex
of a fan, of her womb
my eyes sealed shut, spine curled
like a muslim bowing in a mosque,
bag of blood pressing against my toes,
I tried to jump out, to free myself
but,
I was like a dog tethered to a pole-
that damn umbilical cord!

that damn umbilical cord
pinned me down
like a wrestler pins down his opponent
with an elbow to the jaw
tied me to life, to mother

mother should never have taken that route
to the market, the one covered in dead snails

55

eggshells, and lizard tails-
'cause that's how she met me

II: contemplation
the date of departure is fixed:
I am a mummy,
and I am thankful to every ~~hand~~
knife
that embalmed me

these incisions cannot keep me here
did I not enter this family
with twenty-one birthmarks,
how many more can make me stay?

the date of departure is fixed,
do not tie bells to my ankles
do not anoint my head with olive,
the date of departure is fixed

I do not want to go,
I do not want to go
but death is thinking of me
my friends are thinking of me
I hear them, at night
chanting my name outside the window
they tell me to slip out of my skin,
to come and play in the forest

I miss walking on the edge of leaves
with my fingers,
I miss eating sacrifices placed
at t-junctions,

I miss my wife,
I miss my daughter, Cynthia

mother, I should have gone back
on the day of the naming ceremony,
I should have crawled under
the baby cot to hide, until hunger kills me
until I am emaciated
like plastic cup thrown into fire

but I remember your eyes
how they shone like patent leather in the sun
your warm tears fell on my cheeks that day

so I chose to stay,
a while…

but the date of departure is set
the date of departure is set

who will console
my mother,
who will console the tree without leaves,
who will tell the rat
of the cat in her bosom?

my mother is a leaf,
and I, sickle
my mother is a broken funnel,
in a mechanic's shop
she is a river flowing backwards,
her back turned inwards like a closed book

who will console my mother
when I am gone-
who will take her hands off her head,
who will get her off the floor
when she begins to roll in dust, in grief?

mother, my mother
my tree, hair on my skin
tongue in my mouth, mother, my mother

I will miss you!

songs of woe

"grief is the mother of voyages"
    -   *Romeo Oriogun*

"stories can be heard in the voice of
a cry"
    -   *Joseph Ofejiro Bilabi*

zero is a sound.
of blood seeping
from a vein slashed, a sound
of laughter from a mother's mouth
at the funeral of her child

zero is a sound.
of muttering voices in the wall
at 3am, a sound
of sweat, dragged off
the forehead by the index finger
flung into the air to die

zero is a sound.
of footsteps of the dead
a sound,
of wrinklesbeing deleted
by the scorching feet of the iron:

zero is a sound
heard only by the dead,
a sound
playing deep in my head

song 1

I am roasting.
I am roasting in the flames
that once clothed me

I am melting, my bones
domes of butter
in my body, I am melting
the way eyes melt in obeisance to pepper soup

reproach is a warm towel
around my neck, this fever
is heavy on my brow, this river
-in my head-gallops like a deranged horse;
worse with each breath

a lover once said to me,
for someone who writes a lot about sorrow,
you seem to smile a lot
she does not see my tongue
curled like a cobra, striking my gums,
she does not know that a smile is an adage
told by broken souls

I am roasting, I am melting
a flame dances in my head
my mind shrivels like a frightened pintle
I am beginning to forget places I've been to

I am beginning to spend days
without end, writing
letters to dead lovers

to lovers whose bones are made
of imagination,
whose embrace is but a dream
a wishful thought, all-consuming
like a palm clasping an egg.

Inside my head are two teenage girls
engaged in a pillow fight,
they bicker over little things, like
the time Aunty looked at me too long
at a party- was it with a smirk-
or that day in the dark when a masquerade
rolled my testicles like cowries-
the way an ifa priest consults the oracle

on some days, these girls push me out of my body
and I begin to scream, until the doctors
stab my thighs with tranquilizers

the therapist doesn't understand,
she tells me I have no wife in the otherworld
that there are no girls in my head

but I see them, I see them
two little girls, beating each other up
to survive, two little toads
eating each other up

every.
day.

to survive.

song II

tonight
I tell you the truth,
the moon is a scar on the skin of night

yet, she shines.

I tell you the truth,
the sun is an open wound
on the belly of the sky
and colours gush out in pints

lover, I see you
I see your pain, how you constantly
bite into your lips
in search of water
I see you, stranded in an alley
calling my name, you call so many times
the neighbourhood cats begin to squall

the clouds drift in circles, and the wind
grows a muscle, lifting up mounds of dust
lifting up bones from graves
into the air; a rally of chaos

I cannot answer you.

I cannot answer
because
I am being watched

the psychiatrist is under my bed
the psychologist is in the toilet
the psychiatrist is under my bed

I cannot answer, but what I can do
is break the neck of
of my plastic spoon, and with its edge
draw maps of misery on my laps
so
you can drink. of my blood,

and quench your thirst

for today,
I am the sun.

song III

I want to disappear
like dew in harmattan,
to be transparent
like revolving doors

I like the word *slice,*
how it slips through the lips
without leaving footprints

I hope that the world forgets me
the way a child forgets
early childhood
I want to morph into a pebble
in a bowl of beans
to be picked out, thrown into oblivion
to be forgotten like hair in between joints

tell me, reader
why do you venture into my mind
what do you hope to gain
from my song,

are you a critic, or a potential mimic
 or could it be
that you are salvation
draped in flesh

the earth quivers, leaves fall off a tree
the earth quivers not, leaves
still fall off a tree

every tongue blames the leaf,
every eye eyes the leaf
every foot kicks the leaf
every palm picks the leaf,
only to toss the leaf
into mire

who will face the wind, the thief
caressing every cheek with warmth
yet, shearing every tree in the neighbourhood?

I like the word *slice*...

song IV

the girl of my dreams is hiding
behind my eyes,
knocking on each eyeball
as if to pass a message in Morse code

I nurse cold on many sleepless nights,
wrap myself like a sausage,
reading grand poems of sore sages
whose fingers also knew the meaning
of the word *bleed*
whose palms were icons of self-mutilation

how do you sing yourself to sleep
when your tongue is a serpent?

last night, I saw three red lights in the sky
science textbook says they are old stars
ready to implode

every lover has a tongue
plated with stars
whose expiry date is written
below the bottle of shattered days

song V

when I look into the future
I see my reflection
in a leaf

I write my dreams
on water
so I can forget them quickly

sorrow bends my knees in-
wards, bends my will into a bow
and fires itself into me-
there are broken bottles swimming
in my veins

some nights, when in deep sleep
my fingers turn serpents
and latch onto my wrists

I wake up, to the aftertaste of tears
-in my throat- I wake up
but I am not awake

I am in a room of pictures,
of winking eyes, in a shrine of sour
memories

I look into a picture of myself
hanging on the wall, my mouth is missing
my eyes are missing
the image turns its back towards me, morphs

into a dog with three eyes, a dog
with the tail of a crocodile
and then begins to run
deep into
the
picture

into nothingness, does it think
I cannot follow the trail of memory:

I am betrothed to death
I hear voices, telling me to still
the dam in my chest, to run into nothingness
after the image- otherself-

the orchestra is beautiful, so I say
to them,
"let me amemoir,
I will join you soon"

at the t-junction, I see my wife
garbed in a wedding gown
holding an iroko tree
on its boughs are innumerable hands
waving at me

I try to hide my fear,
the way a lewd monk struggles to cover
a palpable erection, when the nun
touches his shoulder

my wife has only one eye
you will find it
in her belly button,

my wife throws the bouquet
she aims for my throat,
the way an olympian aims his javelin

I stay still, counting my breath
awaiting death-
objects in the future are closer
than they appear

my wife, never blinks…

thorns and petals

"I am a point of light within a greater
light"
-   affirmation of the disciple

rose

*let my cry of pain be crystallized into a little
white fawn,
to run away into the forest!*
-     **Ankh-f-n-khonsu**

I
yesterday,
I saw Rose, washing her tongue
with her mother's hair - a day
after the funeral…

she had shaved a portion of her hair when
no one was looking: now she smells
it every night before she sleeps
in hopes of seeing her mother in a dream

she must be mad,
like me

*sorrow tastes like a worm
sucked out of a bloody eye*

II
roses have ears for petals,
so we drop them on gravestones
to listen to cries we are too afraid to hear

'cause even the earth, with her many fingers
cannot tickle the dead:

but what if we all stopped running, and
chewed our tongues instead

would crying be easier, would
sorrow taste sweeter?

thorns and petals

(for my younger self)

I:on masquerades
yesterday, while picking my nose
I picked a petal
it is true, beautiful things come from dark places

yesterday, while picking a petal
I pricked a finger
it is true, pain is the yolk of beautiful things

many days, I prick my finger digging my nose
there are thorns leaping in my lungs
some, lodged in my liver
others in my spleen

*"Pamilerin, do you know
my grace is sufficient unto you"*
no sir,　　　　no sir
I don't want your thorn in my rectum

there are no petals there…

II: on big aunties with fetishes
god, today
I need your touch

but not like aunty gloria did
when I was in primary two…

aina

enslaved from heaven, she was born with fetters
around
her neck,
a footnote to misogyny in astral planes
that even goddesses can be haunted by their
husbands' ghosts,
in the will it read:
when I go, I will send a helper; my brother
he will lie with you, and lie to you
you will suck on ringworms flowing from his loins
syphilis like milk, death like honey...

she was born with a worm around her neck
a sacred worm, that eats into the brain of a man
whispering to him: daughters are a reproach,
bugs to be squashed like ripe tomatoes
by unwary tires
to be poached like unripe teenagers in a Chibok
reserve

shave your head woman, we want
to etch your husband's name on your skull
stay still little pear, the old bear
who paid your school fees has come
with his turgid sickle, throbbing

be gentle little pea, head between knees
never looking the slave-owner in the eye
his eyes are a gyre of decomposing dreams;
of teenage wives, pillaged from the stem

of urban villages
of teenage dreams, mortgaged for five
tubers of tomorrow…

aina,
divorce is a sin
even when he fondles you with sharp needles

sewing your vulva shut
with hot palm oil and *money for soup,*
milking your eyes of crimson tears

aina,
independence is rebellion;
a good wife

must learn to moan to the thrust
of forced love making

must learn like a dog, to
lick her husband's armpits
in search of foreign scents…

enslaved from heaven, aina was born
with an umbilical cord round her neck
that tightened
every time she tried to tell her husband
she too, was human.

butterfly II
she was a butterfly,
trapped
in the

clench of his fists

well…

she loved it,
till it dawned on her-

he was never alive.

the family eats together
in silence-
father's chair is empty.

dinner

brain freeze

headlines:
"centenarian lynched by mob for being a witch"
"6-year-old burnt alive by irate mob for stealing
kuli kuli"
"comedian, mistaken for cultist executed by mob"
"aluu boys…" wait, old news, old news, hold
that thought

commentary:
when your child steals from the pot,
drag him to the town square
douse him in petrol, and tell
a bystander to light a match

when he tries to run, smack his head
with a crowbar from the carpenter
down the street, so he stays still
so you can enjoy the smell of his skin, roasting.
the scream, aaaahh! that scintillating scream-
1000mg of dopamine injected into your jugular,
tastes like seven full scoops of ice cream
stuffed in your mouth all at once- brain freeze

if he still tries to run, pick up your sins
hide them in stones and   throw
throw until his skull is crushed,
and petals
fall
        out
like spit from a bickering mouth,

target that space between his eyes
and slam a stone into it, as though
aiming for a spider, slam until
his mouth foams like a cup of beer

because he has committed a great treachery
and you,

you are spotless, like a cheetah…

you fool.

water has a voice

we were taught to store our tears
in beer bottles, to break
the head of an emotion with our penis-

what is soft is easily eaten,
easily beaten

we were lectured by mountains
on the secret of hardness, yet untold
of the truth that the skeleton of a rock is water

water has a voice: one should listen to the eyes.
the body is a raging river:
it should be allowed to break into deltas

a little boy hits his toe, blood gushes
pain touches him. he yields:

water has a voice
in the mouth of a child

a man, 27, steps on the eye of a nail
pain touches him. he shrugs:

"I will not remove this nail
until I show all my friends"

for ego, man mutates, becomes
an he-goat
deaf to the voice of water

emotions have gills, you cannot
drown them in water

memory limps, the mind is littered
with shrapnel of the past. african man, your lips
are laced with the hymen of secrets:

we were taught to store our tears
in beer bottles, to keep pain
in the palms of our shadows

in obeisance
        to *manliness*...

the father lets out a yelp
of excitement,
jerks like an epileptic car

as his children are being beheaded
-   **climax (masturbation)**

r&b: rape & beg

(for Mira)
the feet said to the egg,
"I can do no hurt, come,
stay under my heels
she who dwells in the secret place
will abide under the shadow of my almighty..."

but here I am, surfing the internet
picking eggshells off my timeline, thinking:
how do shadows earn the weight of stones?

feet breaks egg, feet rapes egg
feet begins to beg

"but babe, na love I love you o,
I only rapepeople I love,
this your yansh ehn...na die"

little Mira is a fluorescent bulb
glowing in the palm of the night,
the hunter comes with a bat
he says he is after insects, but we know
we can see the bloodlust in his eyes
we know why he swings aimlessly, we know.

hunter breaks bulb, hunter rapes bulb
hunter begins to sob

here I am,
gathering smithereens of Mira's
hymen off the internet- juicy story

84

for online reporters- thinking

where does the light in a fluorescent go
when the shell cracks?

no. is a sacred word

it should be taught
to little girls- and boys-
before the lord's prayer

no.
do not touch me like that.
amen.

to the little one in Syria

many snakes are sucking on your thumb
little one, their tongues-
missiles walking down the isle of Geneva
with the decapitated head of your mother

little one,
your mother's head is a rock from whose ears
soldiers fetched water, for rinsing their butts
after defecating upon the breast of your father
when he whispered *democracy* in Deraa,

and your sister, raped by bullets
dying of thirst
pulled out a vein in her forearm
to drink from, like a straw...

now you wave at the headless ghost
of your mother, wrapped in foreign flags
who promised peace but dropped faeces
on the forehead of Syria

little one, they do not know
that setting fire to a forest does not melt the moon,
that peace is allergic to bullets...

how to forget your heritage

this is how to forget your heritage:

worship the colonists,
wash your skin with acids, to peel off melanin
adopt a nickname: third-world country

demonise the ancestors,
fart in your mother's mouth when she
tries to correct you,
treat your language like vomit

walk through the streets
unclad,
call it freedom

poke the moon in the eye
when it whispers an anecdote

start a revival of your heritage
by building statues, alone

then throw stones at the wind
for chanting your hypocrisy...

profession of faith

god: do you love me,
Jacob?

me: look at my hip.

god: but...*(scratches head)*

me: look. at. my. hip.*(taps hip)*

god: do you love me, Jacob?

me:*(sigh)* look at my hip...

god: alright, please lend me your glasses
it's pretty dark in here

me: no, give me your eyes

god: ok, here you go, you can have it*(hands over
eyes)*

me:*(shoves eyes back into god's hands)*I don't want
your eyes,
I just want you to answer me honestly;
do you,

do you love yourself?

(silence)

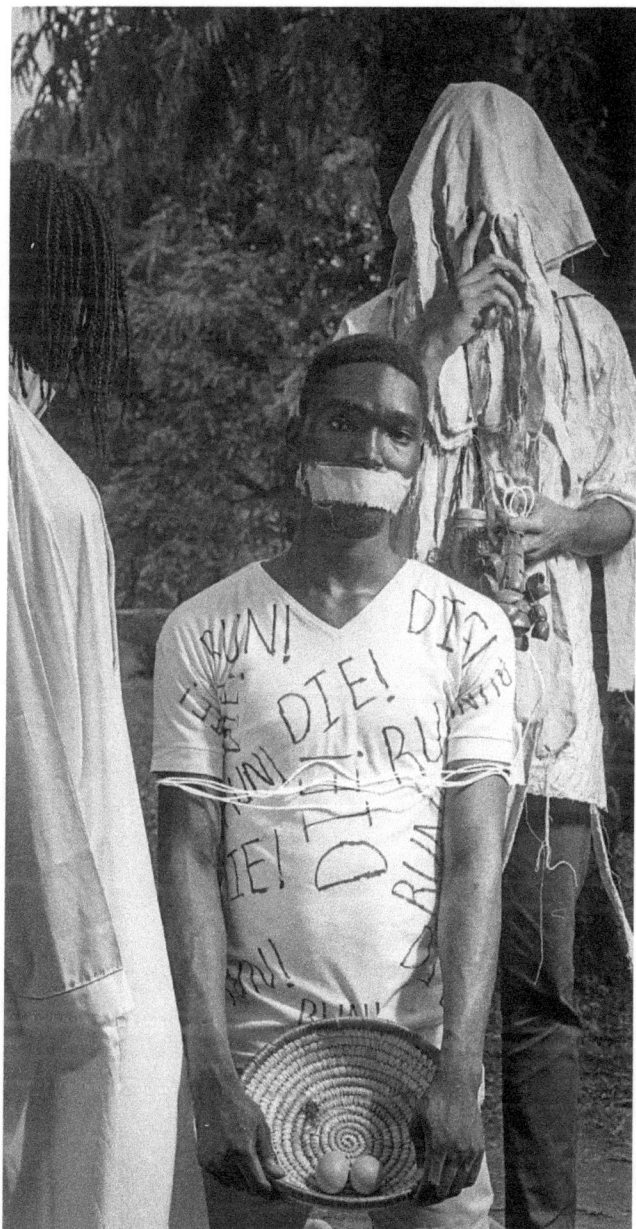

PAMILERIN JACOB is a young Nigerian poet living in Sango-Ota, Ogun State, Nigeria. The major themes in his poems include death, love, abuse, and mental illness. His primary goal of writing is first to ease internal turmoil, and also to shed light on the struggles of mental health patients in Nigeria. Pamilerin has won some local poetry competitions.

His poem was shortlisted for the *Ken Egbas Prize For Festival Poetry* 2017. Pamilerin's writings have featured in the Sprinng Literary Movement 2016 anthology *'These Words Will Cure a Dead Man'* and the 7th issue of the PIN Quarterly Journal, 2017 and WRR Poetry amongst others. Some of his poems will also appear in the Best New African Poets 2017 Anthology set for release in 2018.